MUSIC LESSONS

FLUTE:
GET READY
FOR BAND

by Sarah Broughton Stalbow

First published in 2020 by Best Start Publishing

© Sarah Broughton Stalbow, 2020

ISBN: 978-0-6485764-0-2

The moral rights of the author have been asserted.

All rights reserved. Except as permitted under the Australian Copyright Act 1968 (for example, a fair dealing for the purposes of study, research, criticism or review), no part of this book may be reproduced, stored in a retrieval system, communicated or transmitted in any form or by any means without prior written permission.

All inquiries should be made to the author.

Cover and text design by Sarah Broughton Stalbow, editing by Rob Stalbow.

A catalogue record for this book is available from the National Library of Australia

Best Start Publishing
www.beststartmusic.com

FLUTE: GET READY FOR BAND

This book is especially for students who are beginning to learn the flute as part of a school band program, and particularly those students who are not receiving individual flute lessons. This book is intended to be an integrative resource for the first flute lessons a beginner will receive.

Flutes often have a difficult time in beginner band programs. Unlike some other instruments, it can be challenging to get an initial sound out of the flute. This can be disheartening to young beginners who notice their friends on other instruments making an initial sound with comparative ease. However, this challenge can be overcome by spending time developing a good sound on the head joint, and on a few simple notes, before rushing on to playing the band songs.

The initial focus of the book is on exercises and activities to help a beginner make a sound on the flute. It then goes on to introduce what are arguably the easist notes to play on the flute, working up to the notes commonly used in band songs. A limited number of well known folk songs are used throughout to practise the notes learned - both playing the notes and reading the music. The same songs are repeated in various keys, and also high and low, so that the student systematically learns to play (and read) a large range of notes.

Five and eight note scales are introduced, as well as slurred octaves. These may eventually be used by teachers as warm ups.

It is recommended that beginning flute players practise the embouchure and head joint exercises daily, so that they can develop a beautiful and flexible sound across all registers of the flute.

This book came about after years of encountering students in band programs who did not receive individual lessons. Many of these students struggled with: making a good sound and reading music. Also, they could only play in B flat Major, and had never learned any music other their band songs. For most of these students their teacher (if they had one) had no contact with the parents. Limited communication means that parents often lack the tools and knowledge to assist with practice at home.

Unfortunately, the common characteristic among all these students was that they lacked enthusiasm. I believe that their lack of enthusiasm was a product of their being unable to play their instrument well enough to keep up with their band program, their peers, and the subsequent loss of confidence in their abilities as a music maker. This is a very sad thing to witness, when it could have been easily avoided!

I hope that the exercises and activities in this book will be useful not only for teachers in lessons, but also for students and parents for use at home.

Happy fluting!

Sarah

Contents

Page	
4	Best Start Music Framework
5	For Students
6	Parts of the Flute
7	Reading music
10	Blowing exercises
11	Embouchure exercises
12	Head joint exercises, Tonguing
13	Head joint fundamentals
14	Head joint rhythms
15	Head joint songs
16	Notes B and A
	B and A together
17	Note G; G and A together
	Hot cross buns - G Major
	Au clair de la lune - G Major
	Mary had a little lamb - G Major
18	High Notes: BAG; Octaves (BAG)
	Hot cross buns - G Major (high)
19	Note F; F and G together
	Hot Cross Buns - F Major
	Au clair de la lune - F Major
20	Mary had a little lamb - F Major
	Note F (high)
	Hot cross buns - F Major (high)
21	Note C; B and C together
	Hot cross buns - A minor
	Mary had a little lamb - A minor
22	Note E ; E and F together
	Hot cross buns (starting on mediant)
23	Note B flat; B flat and C together
	F mini (5 note) scale
	Lightly row - F Major
24	The Cuckoo - F Major
	Jingle Bells - F Major

Page	
25	Note D
	D to D finger changes
	D to every other note finger changes
	G mini scale (5 note scale)
	C mini scale (5 note scale)
26	Hot cross buns - B flat Major
	Au clair de la lune - B flat Major
	Mary had a little lamb - B flat Major
	Twinkle twinkle - F Major
27	The Cuckoo - C Major
	Old MacDonald - B flat Major
28	Frere Jacques - F Major
	Lightly Row - B flat Major
29	Low and High D; Three Ds; G mini (5 note) scale); Hot Cross Buns - B flat Major
30	Twinkle Twinkle - B flat Major;
	Happy Birthday F Major
	Frere Jacques - F Major (high)
31	Note E flat
	E flat and F together, E flat and D together; B flat mini scale;
	Hot Cross Buns - E flat Major
32	Frere Jacques - B flat Major
	Twinkle Twinkle - B flat Major
	Happy birthday - B flat Major
33	The Cuckoo - B flat Major
	Old MacDonald - E flat Major
34	Low and High E flat
	Slurred Octaves
	Hot Cross Buns - E flat Major
35	Lightly Row - F Major
	Jingle Bells - F Major
36	C Major scale, F Major Scale, B flat Major scale
37	Crack the Code
39	And finally…

The Best Start Music Framework

Principle →	Develops →	Outcomes
Engagement	Enjoyment Enthusiasm for learning Motivation	
Exposure and varied musical experiences	Musical awareness Knowledge Creativity	**Knowledge**
Routine	Familiarity Learning Strategies Motivation	**+**
Build musical knowledge and correct technique	Musical understanding Literacy Mastery	**Skills**
Small manageable steps	Confidence Enjoyment Secure learning Motivation	**+** **Confidence**
Creativity	Enjoyment Enthusiasm Application Motivation	**+**
Repetition	Consolidates learning Mastery Independence	**Positive sense of self**
Build effective practice habits	Mastery Independence	

Best Start Music Framework (c) copyright Sarah Broughton Stalbow, 2018

"Success is the sum of small efforts repeated day in and day out."

Robert Collier

For Students

Like learning any new skill, playing the flute might feel difficult at first, but if you do a little bit every day it WILL get easier.

There are fingering charts that show you which fingers to use to play the notes in this book.

Wiggle your thumbs, then your first fingers, second fingers, third fingers, then little fingers.

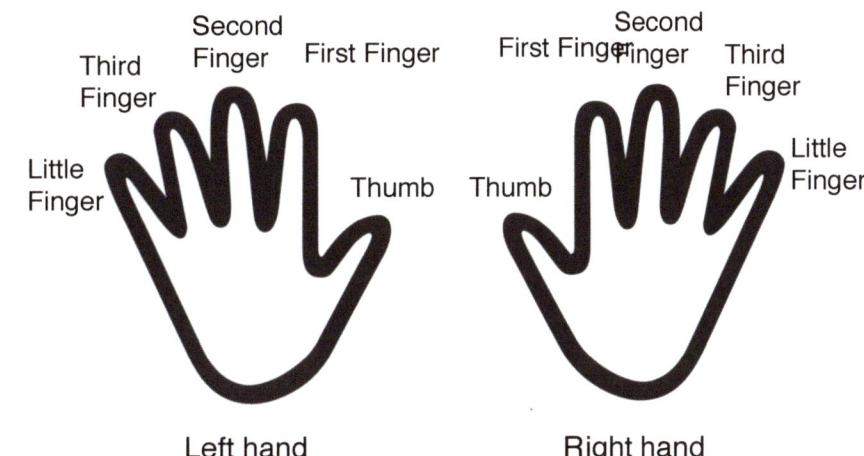

This is a diagram of the flute which shows you which keys to put your fingers on.

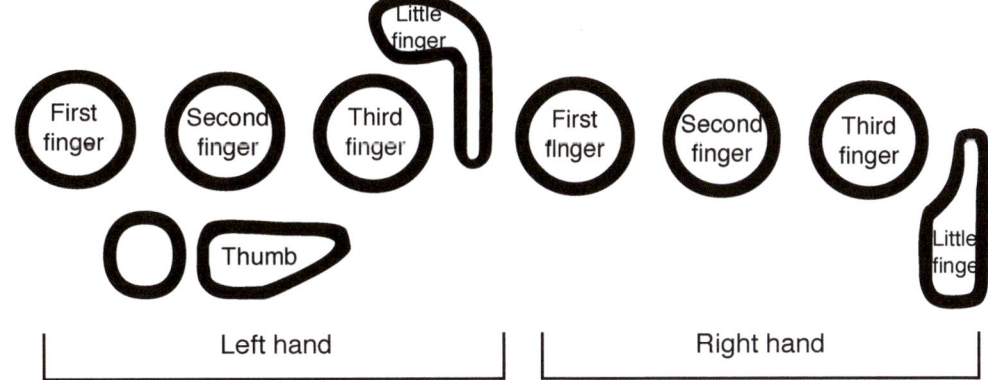

 LISTEN...

- Listen to great flute players every day (find them on YouTube, or ask your teacher for a playlist).
- . Listen to your own sound as you play.
- . Listen to your teacher.
- . Try to copy the good playing you hear.
- . You cannot play well unless you know what playing well sounds like!!

Remember:

A musical instrument is VALUABLE and BREAKABLE.

Treat yours gently or it will break.

Parts of the Flute

Your flute comes in three parts: the **head joint**, the **body**, and the **foot joint**.
The **barrel** is the part of the body that has no keys on it.

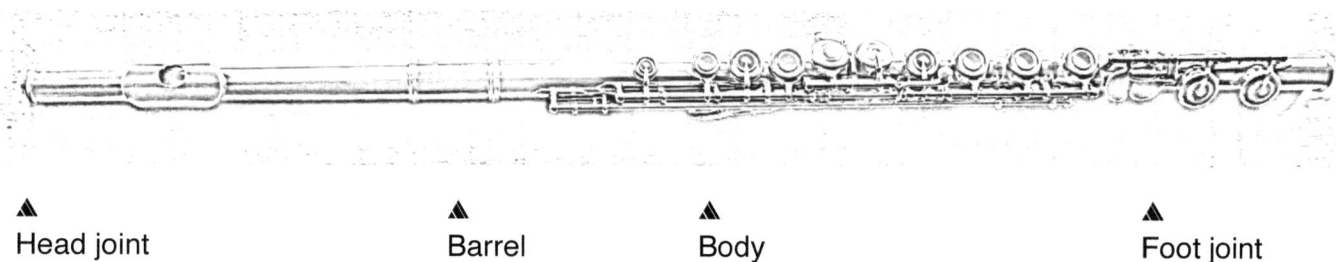

▲ Head joint   ▲ Barrel   ▲ Body   ▲ Foot joint

Hold the flute around the barrel when you put the flute together or take it apart, not around the keys. The keys are delicate and could break with rough handling.

Your flute may have a *straight* head joint (as pictured above), or you may have a *curved* head joint, as shown here.

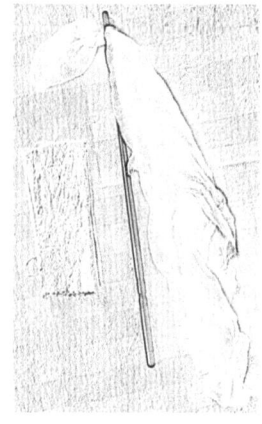

Your flute should come with a **cleaning rod**.
Thread a soft cloth through the hole in the top of the cleaning rod and clean your flute after you play.

Reading music

Music notes are written as symbols which show us how long we hold them for, or how quickly we play them.

RHYTHM is the placement of sounds in time. Here are the most common rhythm symbols.

When you put these symbols together, you create a rhythm!

Symbol	Rhythm name	Notation name	Value
♩	Ta	Crotchet or Quarter Note	1 beat
♪ (half note)	Ta-a	Minim or Half Note	2 beats
dotted half	Ta-a-a	Dotted Minim or Dotted Half Note	3 beats
o	Great Big Whole Note	Semibreve or Whole Note	4 beats
♫	Ti-ti	Quavers or 8th Notes	1/2 a beat each (together makes one beat)
♬♬	Tika-tika	Semiquavers or 16th Notes	1/4 of a beat each (together makes one beat)

In music we use the letters A B C D E F G to name the PITCH of notes.

This is called the **MUSICAL ALPHABET**. Practise saying the musical alphabet forwards and backwards.

PITCH means how high or how low a sound is.

When we reach G in the musical alphabet, we go back to A again.

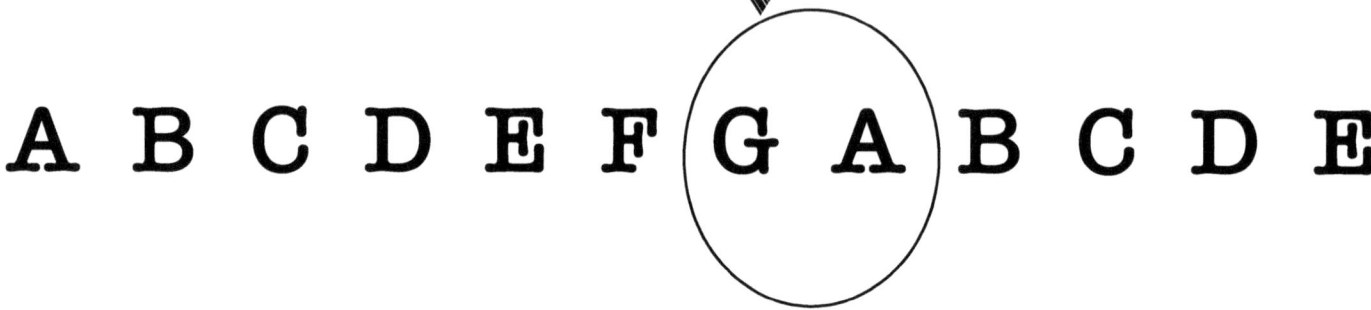

We write music on FIVE LINES and FOUR SPACES.
This is called the **STAFF** (or **STAVE**).

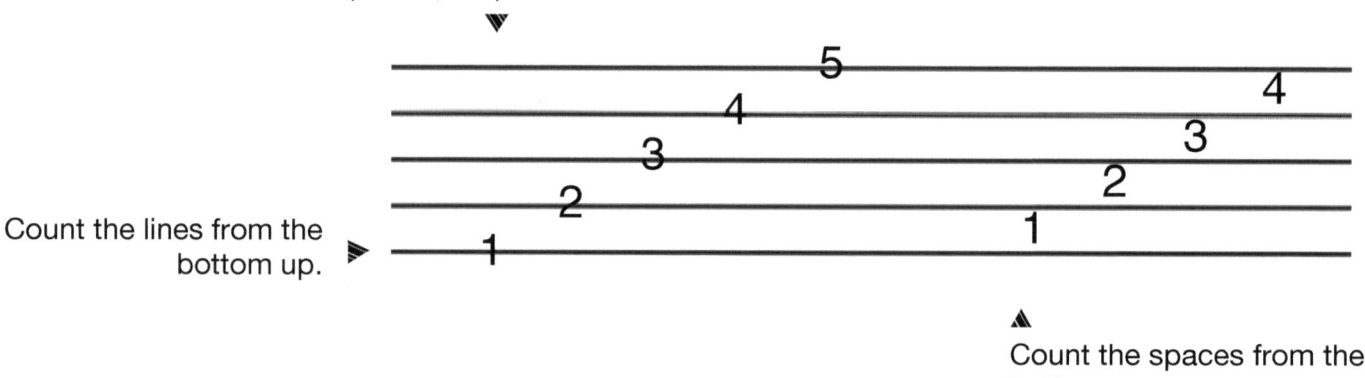

Count the lines from the bottom up.

Count the spaces from the bottom up.

The staff is like a ladder. As we go up the ladder the notes sound HIGHER.
As we go down the notes sound LOWER.

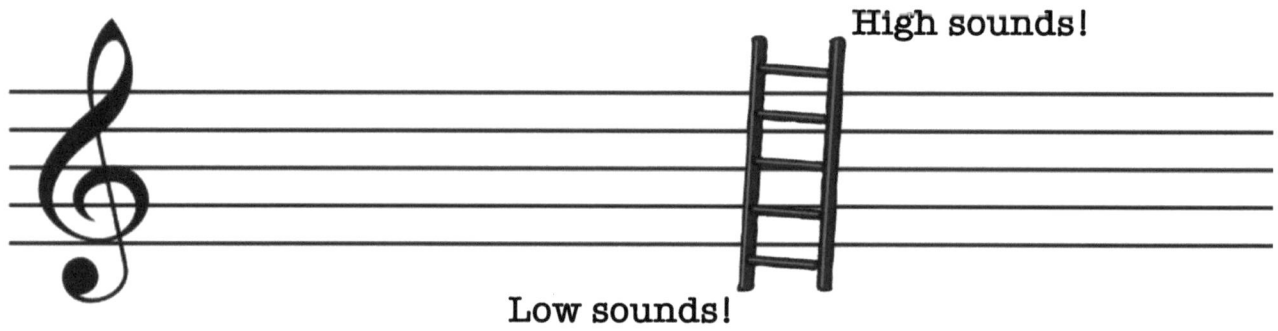

High sounds!

Low sounds!

We write notes on the lines, and in the spaces of the staff.

Line notes are drawn AROUND the line.　　　　　　　　　　Space notes sit INSIDE the spaces.
The line cuts through the centre of the note.

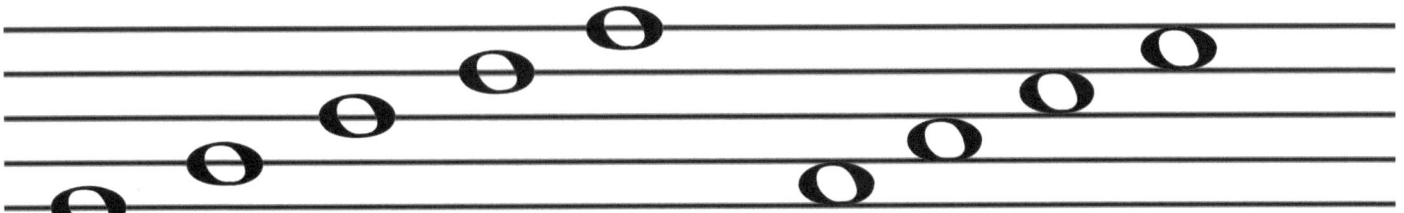

　　This is a TREBLE CLEF.

A treble clef at the beginning of a piece of music tells us that the music is played by an instrument with a high sounding voice.

A treble clef is also known as a G CLEF, because it starts on the G LINE (the second line) and wraps around this line.

You can remember the letter names for the LINE notes like this:

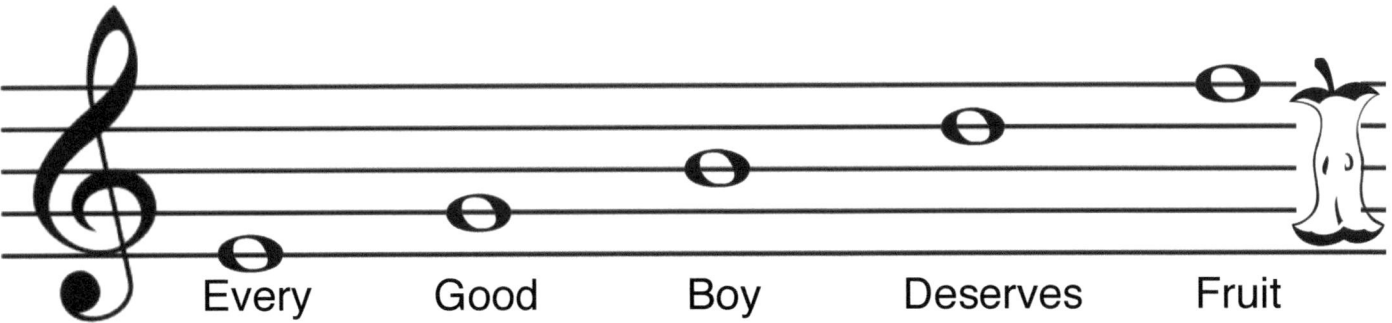

You can remember the letter names for the SPACE notes like this:

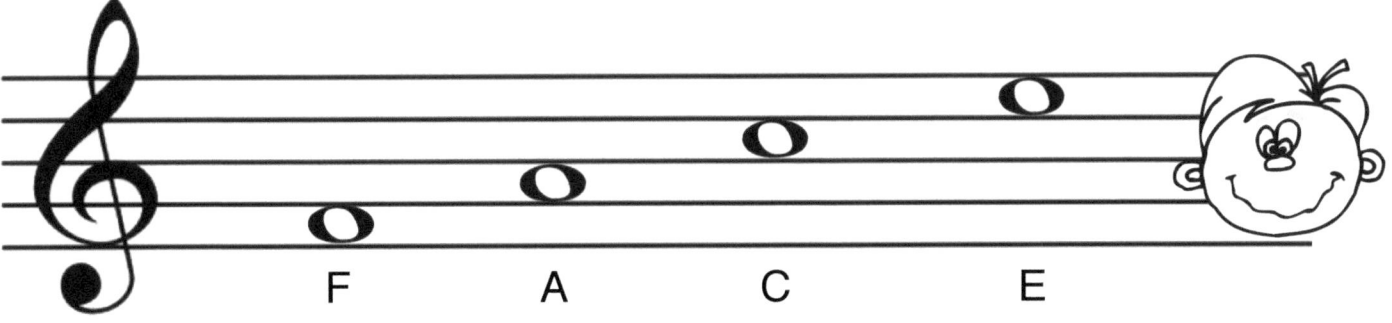

Blowing exercises

Spend A LOT of time on these exercises, the embouchure exercises, and the head joint exercises on the following pages.

This will set you up well for playing with the whole flute put together.

A mirror is your best friend :)

Look in a mirror as you try these exercises.

You will be able to see what works, and be able to fix up what doesn't work.

1. Use a straw
Blow through a straw - feel how the straw goes through the centre of the lips and makes a small hole for you to blow through.

2. Cotton ball races
Using a straw, blow cotton balls across a table or a tray. You can make goal posts and blow the cotton ball through the goal posts to score!

3. A tissue!
Hold a tissue by two corners in front of your mouth. Blow a steady stream of air so the lower edge of the tissue floats upwards. Hold it up with your breath.

4. Look, no hands!
Cut a small square of paper and hold it against the wall. Blow on the paper and take your hands away so that you are holding the paper against the wall with only your breath. Hint: you will need to stand close to the wall.

5. Candle
Blow a candle (real or imaginary!) - just bend the flame, don't blow it out!

6. Windmills
Buy some small windmills (or pinwheels) and blow on them to make them spin.

7. Balloon
Blow up a balloon (or pretend to blow one up). Feel how you use the muscles in centre of your lips (not the corners of your lips or cheeks).

Make a game!

Lay this page flat and throw a die onto it. Do the activity in whichever box it lands the number of times shown on the die.

Embouchure exercises

Embouchure is a French word which describes the shape of the mouth when you blow the flute.

Your lips and cheeks should be in as relaxed and natural a position as possible.

Avoid smiling and tightening the lips and cheeks to make a sound.

See previous page for dice game idea.

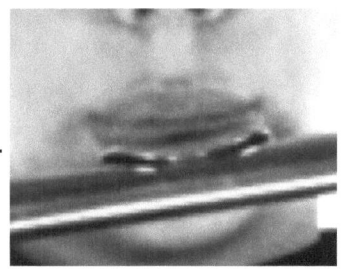

1. Chew like a cow	2. Feel the middle	3. Birthday blowing
Start with lips together. Open and close your teeth keeping your lips together. This will stretch between the top lip and the nose.	Lips relaxed and closed, place your finger on the middle of your lips and feel where the centre is.	Lips relaxed and closed - hold a finger in front of your lips like a birthday candle, and gently blow it through a small hole in the centre of your lips.
4. Up and down air stream	5. The pout	6. The finger pout
Hold your hand in front of your mouth. Blow on the palm of your hand. Without moving your head change the angle of the air stream so you blow on your finger tips, then back to the palm, then blow on your wrist. Work on smoothly blowing up and down your hand from wrist to finger tips and back again.	Pull your bottom lip up over your top lip. 	Put your index finger on your chin, on the edge of your bottom lip. Pout - bottom lip comes up over your top lip. Move your bottom lip down until it lies along your finger… 
7. The blowing pout	8. Rice spitting - 5 parts	9. Rice spitting with finger
Index finger on edge of lip - pout and blow (the air will go upwards). Keep blowing a long stream of air and gradually move your bottom lip down.	1. Breathe in, 2. close mouth, 3. tip of tongue through lips, 4. put a grain of rice on the tip of the tongue, 5. spit the rice off the tongue - 'pop!'	Place your index finger along the edge of your bottom lip and repeat the previous exercise without the grain of rice.
10. Rice spitting plus long air	11. 'P' exercise	12. 'P' exercise on finger.
Place your index finger along the edge of your bottom lip and repeat the rice spitting exercise. However, this time keep blowing a long stream of air after spitting an imaginary grain of rice.	Breathe in, close lips, wait and feel air pressure behind your lips, gently say 'p' to let out a long stream of air out through a tiny hole in the middle of the lips. Aim the air at a point in front of you.	Repeat the previous exercise with your index finger on the edge of your lip. You should be able to hear the sound of the air blowing over your finger.

Head joint exercises

1. Edge of lip
Put your finger on the edge of your bottom lip and feel all the way along its edge. Then, feel where the centre is.

2. Add the head joint
Place the thick edge of the lip plate on your chin with the edge of the embouchure hole (also called the mouth hole) against the edge of your lip.

3. Mirror check!
Your bottom lip should cover roughly a third of the mouth hole (check in a mirror).
Everyone has differently shaped lips and you will need to look in a mirror and experiment with what works best for you.

4. Embouchure exercises
Do the embouchure exercises on the previous page with the head joint in place:
> The blowing pout
> Rice spitting
> Rice spitting with long air
> 'P' exercise
> Birthday blowing
> Up and down air stream

Tonguing

We start each note with the tip of our tongue on the roof of our mouth just behind our front teeth.

1. Say "Too too too" or "Doo doo doo".

2. Whisper "Too too too" or "Doo doo doo".

3. Blow a long air stream on your hand, and move your tongue as you blow: "Too too too" or "Doo doo doo".

4. Start blowing a long stream of air on the head joint, move your tongue "Too too too" as you blow to make separate notes. Don't stop the air between notes!

When you can make a good sound on the head joint, you can move on to the head joint fundamentals on page 13.

Head joint fundamentals

Pick one or two to warm up with each day.

Aim to have played all of them at least once in every week.

Make a game!

Lay this page flat and throw a die onto it.

Do the activity in whichever box it lands the number of times shown on the die.

1. 'Middle' sound	2. 'Low' sound	3. 'High' sound
Head joint - end uncovered. Listen and make the most beautiful, smooth sound that you can. 	Head joint - end covered by the palm of your hand. Slow air stream. 	Head joint - end covered by the palm of your hand. Aim the air slightly upwards and make a smaller hole with your lips to produce a high sound.
4. Spooky sound	5. Long notes	6. Short notes
Move your finger in and out of the end of the head joint while you blow a long stream of air.	How many seconds can you hold a low, middle and high sound for? Write down how many seconds each day.	Use your tongue to start each note. Try using low, middle and high sounds.
7. Tongued notes	8. Helicopter take off	9. Helicopter landing
How many notes can you tongue clearly in one breath? Write down how many each day.	Cover the end of the head joint. Low sound to high sound with one breath (slurring from low to high). Hint: use your lips/jaw to change the angle of the air stream.	Cover the end of the head joint. High to low with one breath (slurring from high to low). Hint: use your lips/jaw to change the angle of the air stream.
10. Head joint rhythms (see page 14)	11. Head joint songs (see page 15)	

Head joint rhythms

Head joint songs

Move your finger in and out of the head joint to play these notes:

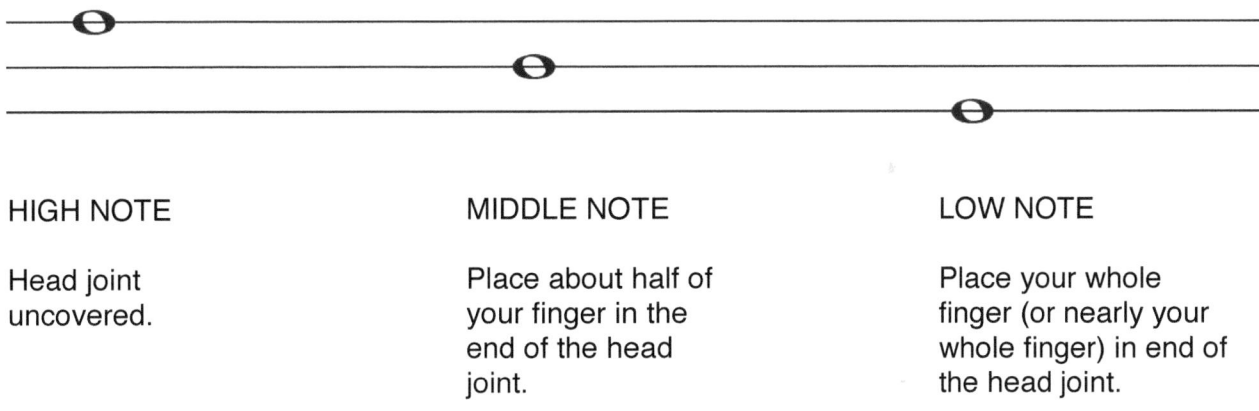

HIGH NOTE	MIDDLE NOTE	LOW NOTE
Head joint uncovered.	Place about half of your finger in the end of the head joint.	Place your whole finger (or nearly your whole finger) in end of the head joint.

Use your ears to tune the notes and play the following songs:

Hot Cross Buns - head joint only

Mary had a little lamb - head joint only

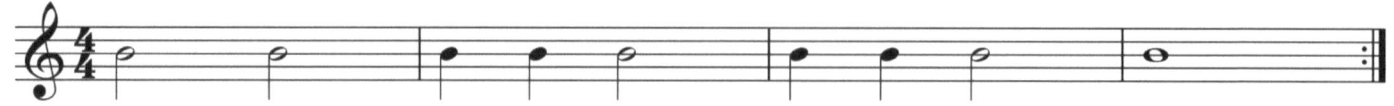

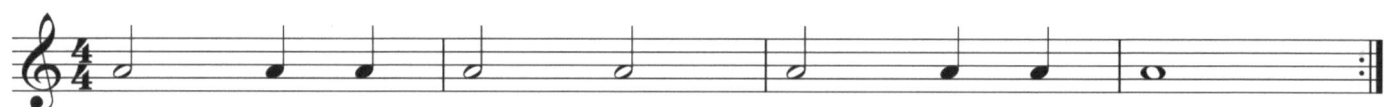

B and A together

G

Hot Cross Buns

Au Clair de la Lune

Mary had a litte lamb

High Notes

These high notes have the same fingering as their respective low notes.

G

A

B

Octaves

1

2

3

4

5

6

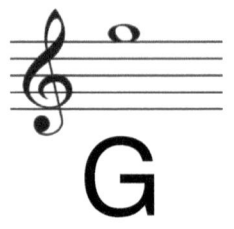

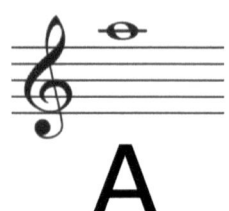

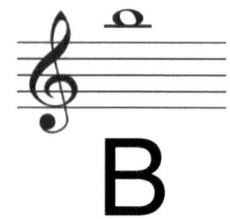

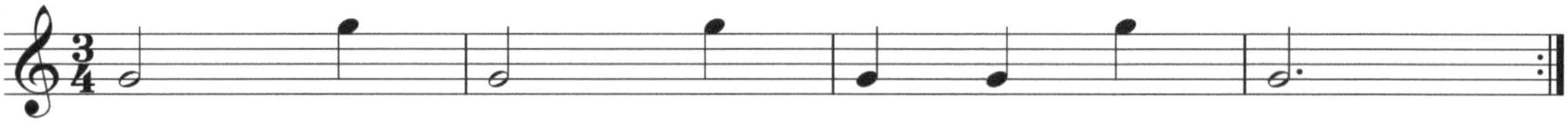

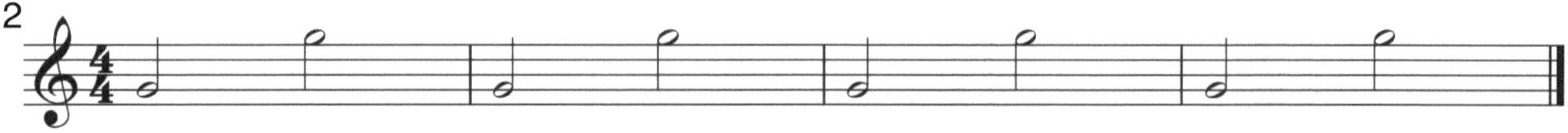

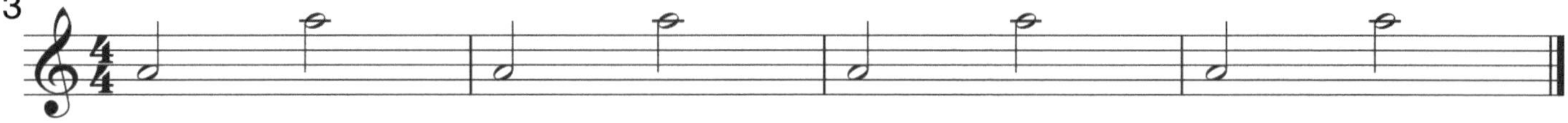

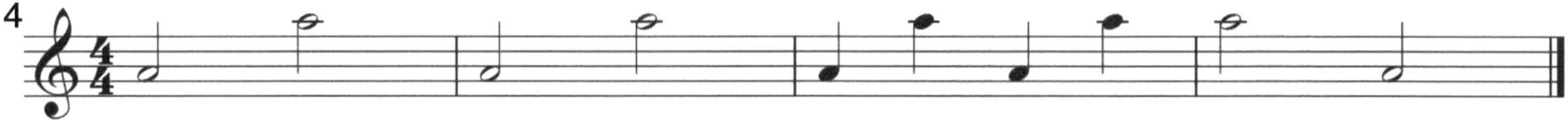

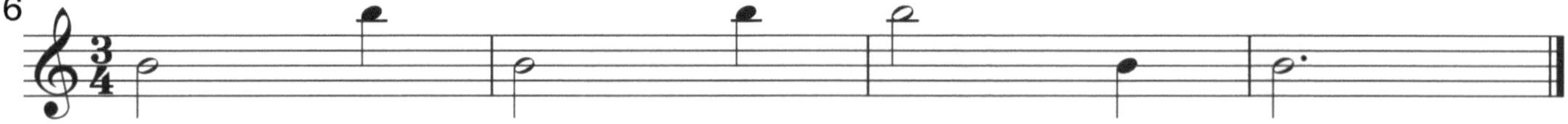

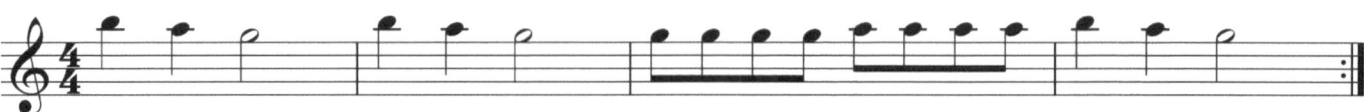

Hot Cross Buns (high notes)

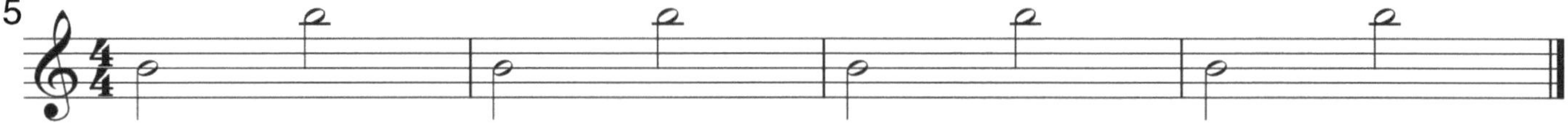

F

G and F together

Hot Cross Buns - F Major

Au Clair de la Lune - F Major

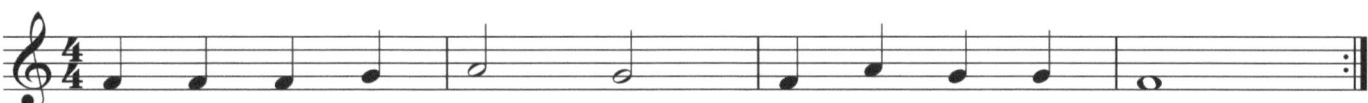

Mary had a little lamb - F Major

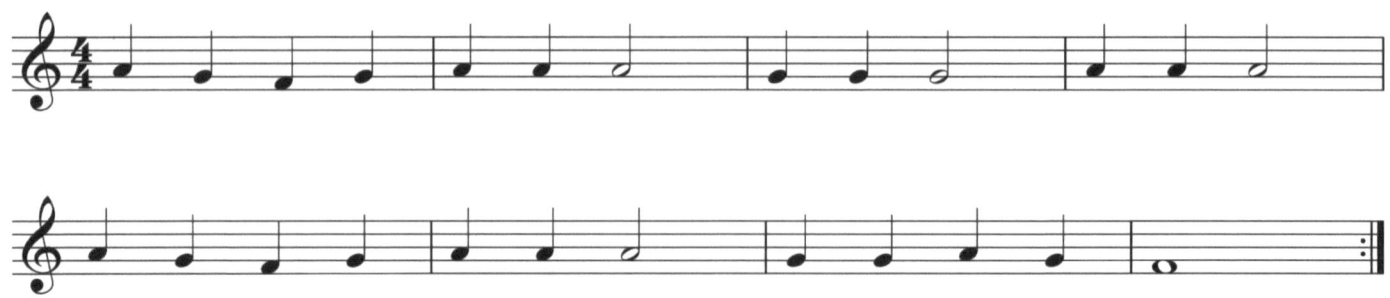

High note F

F Octaves

Hot Cross Buns (high) - F Major

C

B and C together

Hot Cross Buns - a minor

Mary had a little lamb - a minor

E

Low E and high E have the same fingering.

F and E together

Hot Cross Buns - starting on mediant (low and high)

B♭

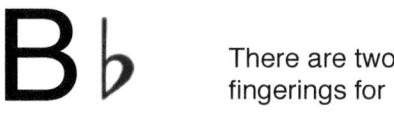There are two fingerings for B flat

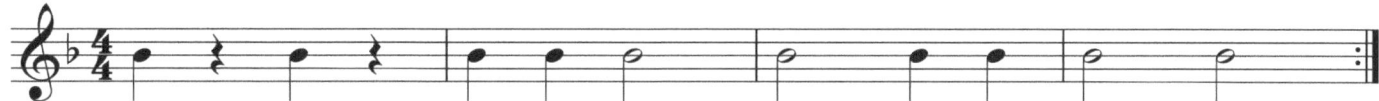

B♭ and C together

F mini scale (5 note scale)

Lightly Row - F Major

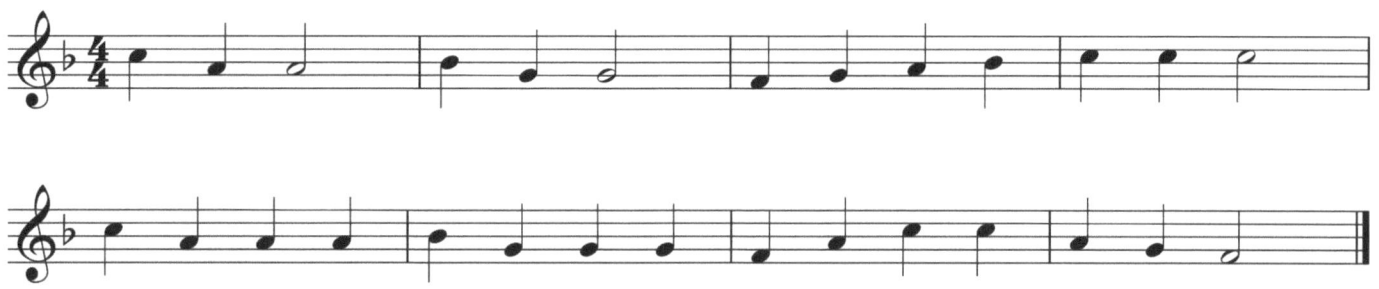

The Cuckoo - F Major

Jingle Bells - F Major

D

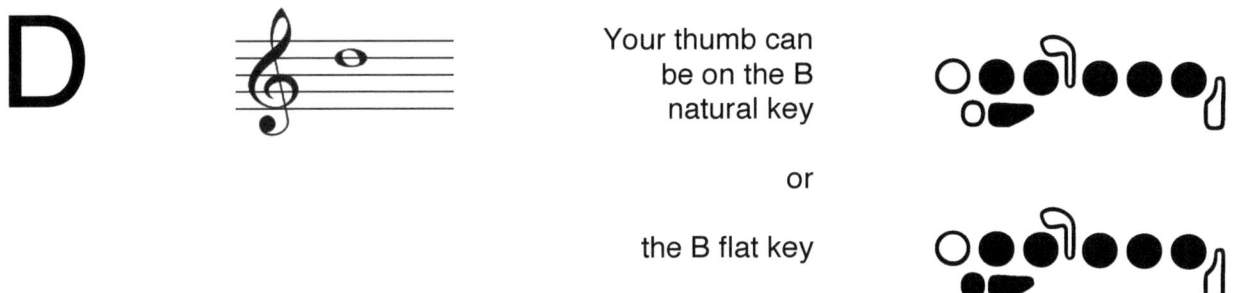

Your thumb can be on the B natural key

or

the B flat key

C to D finger changes

D to every other note finger changes

G mini scale (5 note scale)

C mini scale (5 note scale)

Hot Cross Buns - B♭ Major

Mary had a little lamb - B♭ Major

Au clair de la lune - B♭ Major

Twinkle Twinkle - F Major

The Cuckoo - C Major

Old MacDonald - B♭ Major

Frere Jacques - F Major

Lightly Row - B♭ Major

Low and High D

Your thumb can be on the B natural key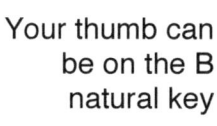

or

the B flat key

Three Ds

G mini scale (5 note scale - high)

Hot Cross Buns - B♭ Major (high)

Twinkle Twinkle - B♭ Major (high)

Happy Birthday - F Major

Frere Jacques - F Major (high)

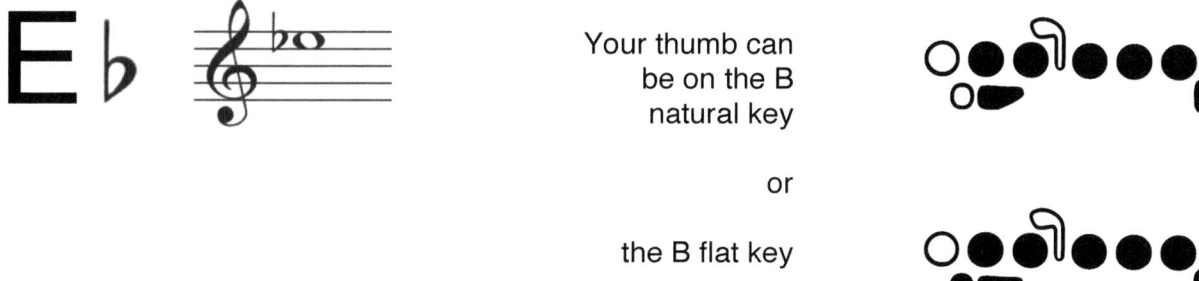

E♭ and F together

E♭ and D together

B♭ mini scale (5 note scale)

Hot Cross Buns - E♭ Major

Frere Jacques - B♭ Major

Twinkle Twinkle - B♭ Major

Happy Birthday - B♭ Major

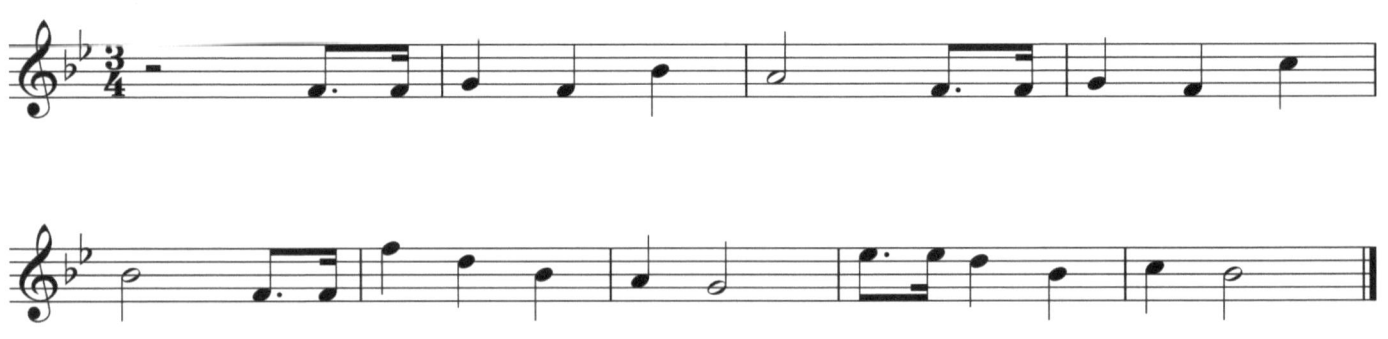

The Cuckoo - B♭ Major

Old MacDonald - E♭ Major

Low and High E♭

Your thumb can be on the B natural key

or

the B flat key

Octaves - ascending

These curved lines are called *slurs*. Play the notes under the slur smoothly, without tonguing.

Octaves - descending

Hot Cross Buns - E♭ Major (low)

Jingle Bells - F Major (high)

Lightly Row - F Major (high)

8 Notes Scales

C Major

F Major

B♭ Major

Crack the Code

Write the letter names under the notes to spell words.

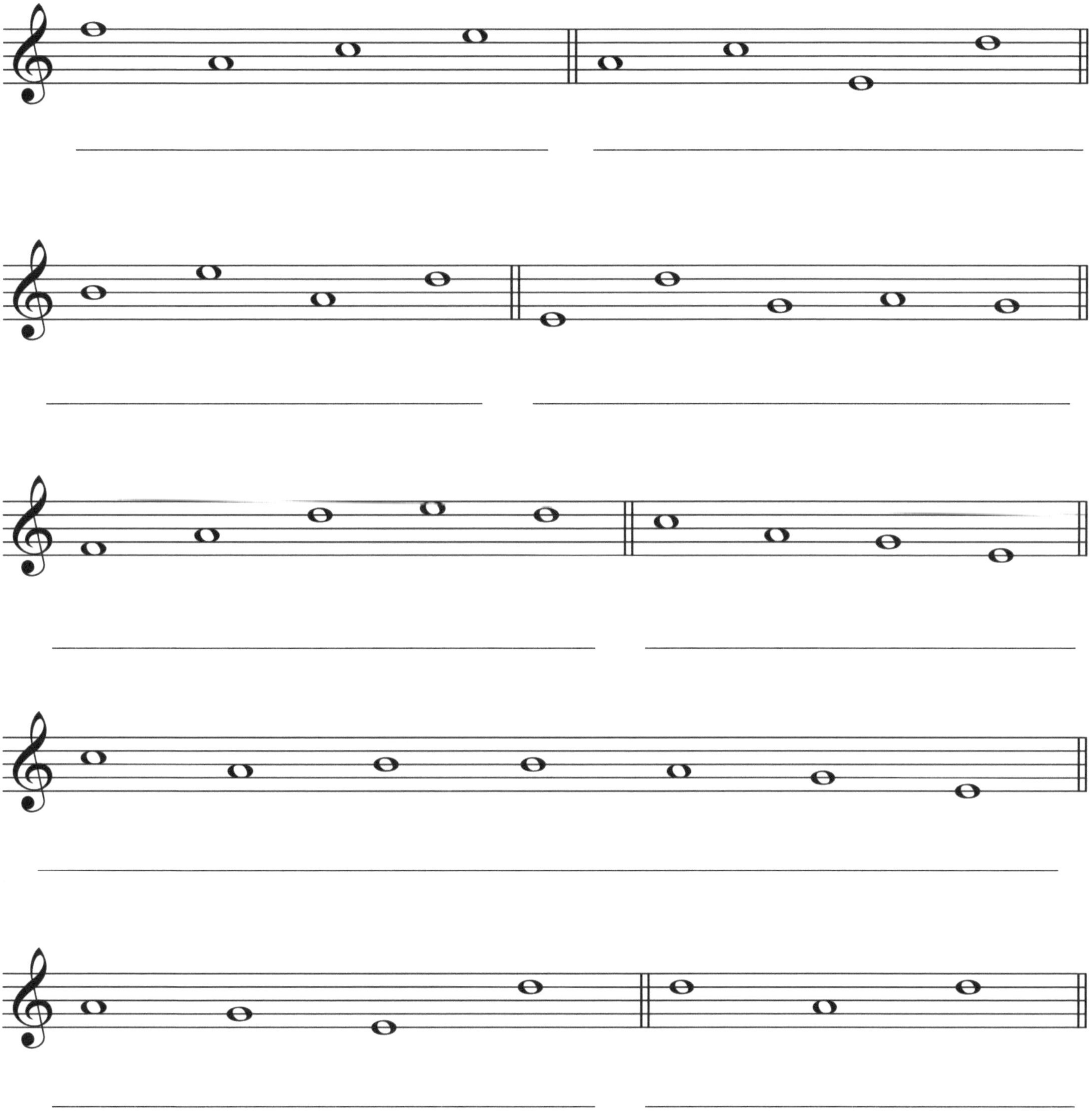

Crack the Code

Write the letter names under the notes to spell words.

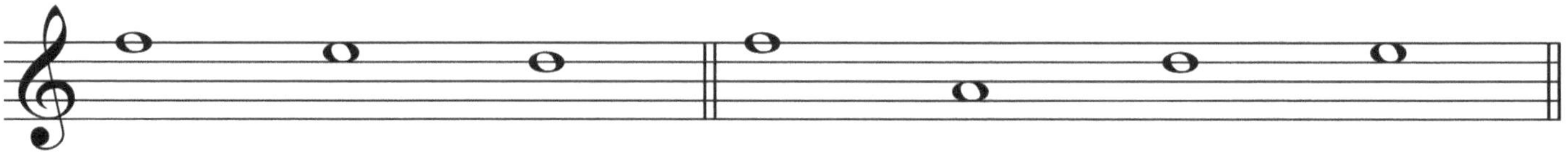

And finally...

Person: How do you perform so well?

Musician: Practice

Person: It must be an innate gift...

Musician: It's Practice.

Person: I can never understand why some people have talent like this. It's magical and a mystery.

Musician: It's practice.

From Classic FM on Twitter
@ClassicFM
The official Twitter home of Classic FM, the UK's favourite classical music station

www.ingramcontent.com/pod-product-compliance
Lightning Source LLC
Chambersburg PA
CBHW041428010526
44107CB00045B/1533